BUZZWORDS

———————▶

DIRECTING YOUR MIND
TO HEALTH, HAPPINESS,
AND FULFILLMENT

GLORI GAGE

Copyright © 2022 Glori Gage

All rights reserved. No part of this book may be reproduced or transmitted in any form or by any means without the express written consent of the copyright owner, except for the use of brief quotations in a book review.

To request permissions, contact the publisher at
publisher@glorigage.com
www.glorigage.com

ISBN: 978-1-7780528-3-5 [Paperback]
ISBN: 978-1-7780528-2-8 [KPF]
ISBN: 978-1-7780528-1-1 [EPUB]

First edition
Editor Jennifer Kepler
Proofreader Amanda Kruse
Cover design by Damonza
Formatting by Polgarus Studio
Back cover photo courtesy of the Author

This book is dedicated to those individuals who want to empower themselves to be the best they can be and to live life to its fullest.

Whatever we plant in our subconscious mind and nourish with repetition and emotion will one day become a reality.

—Earl Nightingale

CONTENTS

PREFACE xi

INTRODUCTION xiii

LIFE 1

    Perfectly Unperfect 3
    Free to Be 4
    For Change, Make Change 5
    Move It Forward 6
    Fascinating 7
    Do My Part 8
    Choice, Not Chance 9
    Listen Closely 10
    Not the Right Fit 11
    Be Prepared 12
    Plan B 13
    What's Yours Is Yours 14
    Feel Hard Feelings 15
    I Am Safe 16
    Not Mine to Own 17
    Due Diligence 18
    Step Up…Speak Up 19
    Be Grateful 20
    Walk the Talk 21
    Be Me 22

- Let Life In 23
- Find the Joy 24

RELATIONSHIPS 25
- Dig Deeper.. 27
- Be Brave 28
- Respect Difference...................................... 29
- For the Team 30
- Dark Cloud 31
- Stop Bullying Me 32
- All I Have... 33
- Not My Issue 34
- Building, Not Breaking 35
- This Is Hurtful 36
- At Arm's Length 37
- Pushing Rope 38
- It's Me.. 39
- Forgive Them... 40

PARENTING...41
- I Am Listening 43
- Two-Way Street 44
- House Rules 45
- Give Them Tools 46
- I Believe in You 47
- Convince Me.. 48
- Need Your Help 49
- Let Them Lead 50
- Store Is Closed 51
- Teaching Moment...................................... 52

Love Them More 53

CHILDREN 55
Be the Best Me 57
I Am Loved 58
Not My Thing 59
Journal 60
Only One Chapter 61
Think of Others 62
Ouch, That Hurt 63
Not Right 64
Free to Be Me 65

HEALTH 67
Honour Thy Body 69
Trust Mother Nature 70
Fix What's Broken 71
Eat Right 72
Quality, Not Quantity 73
Food, Not Filler 74
Breathe One, Two, Three 75
I'm a Cadillac 76
Fill Me with Light 77

SPIRITUAL 79
Honour Thyself 81
God's Plan 82
Rejoice Always 83
Feed Your Soul 84
God Wink 85

I Am Blessed	86
Stretch Me	87
In God's Hands	88
Here I Am, Lord	89
Angel on Earth	90
Keep the Faith	91
My Purpose	92
WORKPLACE	**93**
Read the Signs	95
Take the Initiative	96
Head in the Game	97
Absolutely	98
Need to Fuel	99
Great Work	100
Not Appropriate	101
Don't Sell Out	102
Red Flag	103
Money Isn't Everything	104
BUZZWORD TOOLBOX	**105**
ACKNOWLEDGMENTS	**113**
RESOURCES	**117**
ABOUT THE AUTHOR	**121**

PREFACE

I had been struggling in my life for quite some time. I was lost and overwhelmed, and I did not know where to turn. I was looking for an answer and, oddly enough, found it on a subway billboard advertising courses in philosophy. It was in taking these classes that I learned new ideas, thoughts, and tools that would ultimately change my state of mind and help move me forward in my life. I learned that my mind is a powerful instrument, and I have the power to redirect it positively and proactively. I was inspired to look at mental notes, or what I would come to call "buzzwords," when I was struggling or needing a push in the right direction.

These buzzwords would be used to shift my thinking. They moved me out of my state of angst and stress, bringing me balance, clarity, direction, and peace of mind. As I continued to add new buzzwords, I became more empowered knowing that I could look to myself for answers.

You have the same power, for each of us controls our state of mind. I have written this book to inspire you with positive and proactive buzzwords that can help change the direction of your thinking and, in turn, change the course of your life.

INTRODUCTION

As children, many of us can remember hearing mindful reminders, or what I now call buzzwords, to keep us focused on the important things. When heading out to school, we would hear "Don't talk to strangers." Before crossing the street, we'd be told, "Look both ways." If we were visiting a friend's home, we would hear "Mind your manners" and "Say thank you." Or when playing games, "Play by the rules," "Play fair," and "Don't forget to share." This essential messaging was an excellent way for our parents, caregivers, teachers, and anyone else in our midst to ingrain into our wee minds a valuable tool to keep us safe, healthy, and socially acceptable.

Our mind is like a supercomputer, which we can program. What we put in is what we get out. Each one of us has the power to program our minds in any direction we choose. With the multitude of negative messages in our world, it is vital for our overall health and well-being that we redirect our minds to positive and proactive messaging. Our thoughts influence our attitudes and, in turn, our actions and reactions. By choosing positive thoughts and mastering our state of mind, we empower ourselves to experience greater health, happiness, and fulfillment.

Buzzwords are valuable tools that can help us throughout life. Maybe you're trying to focus on a specific goal or you want to change a negative mental habit. A buzzword must resonate with you—you must believe in it, honour it, and be able to repeat it, either internally as a thought or out loud for others to hear.

The buzzwords I have included in this book are positive and proactive. Negative buzzwords do not, I repeat, do not, bring about the rewarding changes that you are searching for. Positive energy attracts more positive energy.

I have divided this book into seven sections: *Life, Relationships, Parenting, Children, Health, Spiritual,* and *Workplace*. However, many of the buzzwords in this book can apply to all areas of your life. I've also included additional, "standard" buzzwords in a *Buzzwords Toolbox* at the end of the book; these are important ones we all know and are likely already using on a regular basis.

To start the journey that can change your life in the most enriching and profound way, look at the specific section that you are most in need of changing. For example, turn to the *Life* section to motivate and inspire you in your day-to-day living. Look at the *Relationships* section to help you nurture your relationships in a whole new way. Turn to the *Children* section to help a child or the inner child in you. Then find one, yes, just one, buzzword that fits. Memorize it, repeat it often, and embed it in your mind. When the moment arises, use the selected buzzword to motivate and inspire you or help defuse a situation.

As you see the positive ways a buzzword can impact your life, start using other buzzwords or create new ones of your own. Once you have mastered the use of buzzwords to direct your thinking in a positive way, you will be empowered in all areas of your life. I believe every one of us has the power to change and love our lives. Buzzwords will help initiate this change and move you forward to a new state of happiness, success, joy, and fulfillment. You have that power with buzzwords!

LIFE

We are intricate beings, and we are moved in many ways by internal and external forces. It is not easy navigating through the day-to-day challenges, struggles, and triumphs that are a part of our journey. We are all unique in how we process the many things that we experience; for some, those things can strengthen and move us forward, and for others, they can paralyze us and stop us in our tracks.

Each of us has the power within to reprogram our state of mind and change the direction of our life. These *Life* buzzwords are ones to help motivate, break negative habits, repel negativity, and most importantly, calm and empower us with the knowledge that these new tools will always be there to call upon for guidance.

Perfectly Unperfect

OK, I admit that I am a perfectionist. I love working hard to pull everything together, place it gingerly in a little box, and adorn it with a beautiful bow. But as we know, life does not work that way, and as much as I might try to put something or someone into "my little box," it is not always easy or pretty. Hence, when I thought of this buzzword, I ran to my computer, typed it in, and prayed for that red line indicating that the words "perfectly unperfect" were not grammatically correct. When this indeed happened, I screamed "YES!" and triumphantly fist pumped into the air.

What makes this buzzword perfect is the contradiction of the words—something being perfectly unperfect. This buzzword is great to use when we need to recognize that perfection is not always attainable. So, when you've done the best you can but you're still not satisfied, look to "Perfectly Unperfect" as a buzzword to help you step out of the situation, accept that not everything can be perfect, and find peace with it.

Free to Be

In this new age of information overload, it is easy to find an expert on or opinion about everything, and I mean everything! Even before you have had a chance to think for yourself, someone is telling you what to do. It is essential to our well-being that we shut out this noise so we can journey inward to find our true selves. We know what makes us laugh, what foods fuel our bodies, which people energize us, and what inspires us.

We are all beautiful and unique individuals, and we each contribute to this world by what we share of ourselves. Honour this in yourself and in others, for in doing so, you will experience great freedom and joy and will make this world a better place. When you question what you know to be real and true, use the buzzword "Free to Be" to find the strength to be your true self.

For Change, Make Change

It is always easy to say we want to change our lives, but it is actually hard to do. We are creatures of habit, and once we are comfortable in a rhythm, be it good, bad, or ugly, we like to stay there. It takes an asserted amount of effort and energy to change our path.

The buzzword "For Change, Make Change" is one that calls for *action*. It is a mental prompt to make a change in our lives, to do something different, be it emotional, physical, or spiritual. We have the power to shift our state of mind, which allows us to make this change. Taking the first step by making a change in a positive direction can open our world in a whole new way.

Move It Forward

In life, we experience wonderful, enriching moments and challenging ones. It is these challenging experiences that can weigh us down like accumulating baggage. We need to sift through these experiences to find answers, clarity, understanding, and hopefully, a resolution, if not with others, then at the very least with ourselves. We need to forgive ourselves and others for what we did not know at the time and collect new knowledge along the way, like gold nuggets of wisdom. So, as this buzzword suggests, "Move It Forward."

It is not *what* happens in life but what we *do* that builds and strengthens us. Yes, there will always be a period of time that needs to be respected as we sort through any given situation and those feelings attached to it, but then action must be taken. Do not let events define and paralyze you, as it is in the moving forward after adversity and struggle where real growth and success happen.

Fascinating

In my everyday life, I find I can become emotionally invested in negative interactions with others that have nothing to do with me. Whether it be the expression on their face or the words they use, their message is loud and clear.

I have found that using the buzzword "Fascinating" allows me to mentally step out of a situation and observe it without personal and emotional attachment, which helps me recognize it is about them and not me. The ability to step out is not only fascinating but also freeing, as we do not have to take ownership of someone else's negative and misdirected behaviour.

Do My Part

Each one of us has a responsibility to ourselves, others, and this incredible world in which we live to do our part. We are just one part of the greater whole, and what we do individually affects others and this planet we share.

The current health of our planet is an example of why we need to listen and take action. Presently, it is calling upon us to make changes to our throwaway society and the staggering amount of garbage we generate. Each year, approximately eight million metric tons of nonbiodegradable plastic end up in our oceans. With this knowledge, each one of us can direct our minds to do our part by reducing the amount of plastic we use.

On a small scale, we can purchase goods in glass or compostable paper rather than plastic, expand our use of reusable drinking bottles, and use washable nonplastic grocery bags. On a larger scale, we can purchase goods only from companies that are actively doing their part, and most importantly, we can vote for a government that will commit to implementing laws that benefit our planet. Each one of us must make a conscious effort to be part of the solution and not the problem, so take action with the buzzword "Do My Part."

Choice, Not Chance

One of my favourite books is *Life's Greatest Lessons: 20 Things That Matter* by Hal Urban. It has been a constant go-to book throughout my life, for Urban shares his insights and wisdom in such an honest and open way. Written initially for his children and his students, he, as a father and teacher, shares what he believes are the important lessons to living a fulfilled life.

Chapter 4 of his book, titled "We Live by Choice, Not by Chance," is what inspired the buzzword "Choice, Not Chance." I found this chapter exciting and liberating, as it helped me attain freedom and strength with the knowledge that each of us has the ability to choose. The buzzword "Choice, Not Chance" directs us to the knowledge that our lives and the decisions we make about how we live our lives are in our very own hands.

Listen Closely

I believe many of us may feel that we always listen, but today, when our brains are busy doing so many things at once, we do not really listen. The buzzword "Listen Closely" reminds us to be here in the moment, take a breath, and pause to listen to all that life truly has to offer. Our universe is a magnificent place, and it is teaching us every day, through nature, through our bodies, and through our interactions with others.

In life, listening closely can help us experience moments in ways that enrich and fulfill us. With our bodies, listening closely helps us hear the warning signs that our intricate and amazing bodies are telling us. In our relationships, listening closely helps us reconnect and rediscover each other.

This buzzword applies not only to the words that are spoken but also to what is not said or what one's body language is telling us. When we are truly present for ourselves, we can be fulfilled and bring harmony to our body, mind, and spirit. When we are truly present for others, we can make them feel loved, respected, supported, and valued.

Not the Right Fit

There are times in life when something just does not work. You don't know why, but you can feel it. You may take lots of time searching for a reason but just cannot put your finger on it, and no matter how hard you try, it's not going to work.

It is at these times, when you can feel it in your bones and you need some sort of resolution, that the buzzword "Not the Right Fit" can direct you to a new way of thinking. It's clean and straightforward, as it will help you recognize that you are wasting valuable time and energy on something that is, in the end, just "Not the Right Fit."

Be Prepared

I was never a Girl Scout, but I have always loved their motto: "Be prepared." We cannot prepare for everything in life, but there are many things that we can do. In my case, for example, it seems our car prefers me to be behind the wheel when it gets a flat tire.

The first time this happened to me, I was driving alone on a country road, racing to get to a lunch date, and the next time, when racing to get home with a birthday cake where a houseful of guests was soon to arrive. In the latter case, my first impulse was to continue to drive no matter what damage I was doing to the wheel. Thankfully, I chose not to, as my husband had once informed me that if I did drive with a flat tire, resulting in the unnecessary expense of a new wheel, I should not expect a warm welcome when I arrived home!

With this buzzword, "Be Prepared," I learned how to change a tire. Yes, I could just call roadside assistance, but I wanted to be able to do it myself. Now, the stress of worrying about the next time I get a flat tire has been washed away by this newfound knowledge of being prepared.

There are many things that we put off doing or learning, whether it be implementing a time-saving task, learning a lifesaving skill, or just planning for the future. Yes, these things are not always easy to do, but once completed, we feel a fabulous sense of accomplishment, independence, and empowerment…"Be Prepared!"

Plan B

Having a goal or plan to work toward in life gives us purpose; it motivates and drives us forward. However, if you are someone who gets discouraged and becomes paralyzed when your plans do not materialize or unfold as you wish, then the buzzword "Plan B" is for you.

There is an old saying, "When one door closes, another opens," so trust that, in life, there will be times we must modify or change our plans. This buzzword will inspire you to refocus your mind and energy and help move you in a new direction.

What's Yours Is Yours

It was while traveling in Europe, when over a glass of wine and in deep conversation about the personal affluence that we were seeing all around us, that the words "What's yours is yours" came up in reference to how one can view other people's state of wealth, privilege, or position. To me, it seems to be a healthier philosophy than our North American "keeping up with the Joneses" mentality.

The buzzword "What's Yours Is Yours" moves us away from comparison and helps us acknowledge and celebrate others' success without any thought to ourselves. OK, I know this is easier said than done, especially with the magnitude of comparisons made, given the constant barrage of information through advertisements, social media, and the internet. But being locked in a state of envy is not a healthy thing.

We must redirect our minds to a healthier perspective and move away from the preoccupation with other people's lives so we can concentrate on living our own. So, in times of envy or wanting what others have, utilize the buzzword "What's Yours Is Yours" to help redirect your energy and state of mind to living your *own* life, and celebrate all that you are and all that you have.

Feel Hard Feelings

We are programmed to try to omit the pain of life whenever possible. If we have a headache, our first impulse is to reach for pain-relief medication when, in fact, our body may simply require some food, water, or a much-needed break. If struggling in a relationship or more serious matters of the heart, we may find it easier to bury or ignore emotions than talk about them.

What we fail to understand is that pain is part of what makes us human and is a natural part of life. It is our alarm system that tells us when something is out of balance and needs attention, and it drives us to new heights in our understanding of ourselves and empathy for others.

As science has proven, a broken bone is stronger once it has mended. I am not saying one needs to break a bone, but when faced with adversity, difficulty, or suffering, face it—feel it and grow from it. The buzzword "Feel Hard Feelings" will help you realize that these emotions are a natural and vital part of life.

I Am Safe

At times in our lives, we may find ourselves in toxic and unhealthy situations. Sometimes we can remove ourselves from them, but other times, we cannot. It is at these times, when we cannot remove ourselves, when we get drawn into this turmoil, that the buzzword "I Am Safe" can redirect our minds inward to our inner core, inner strength, and inner calm.

This buzzword is a powerful one, for it can help when we feel that we are spiralling and need reassurance that we can regain our footing. "I Am Safe" can give us the confidence and calmness that we can manage this situation or find the inner strength needed to look to outside resources that are available to us.

Not Mine to Own

This buzzword is a special one, for it was my very first! While attending a philosophy class, I came to a new understanding of myself and others. I learned that everyone has their own journey in life, and each person must do their own work.

The class instructor shared that it is in making the decision and doing the work that we develop our sense of self and confidence so we can take responsibility for the choices in our lives, which is essential to our personal growth and well-being. That made perfect sense to me, and with this realization, it inspired me to create "Not Mine to Own." I call upon this buzzword regularly to remind myself to be supportive and encouraging of others but not take on their decision-making or their work, for it is "Not Mine to Own."

Due Diligence

When something sounds too good to be true, in most cases, it is just that: not true! It is always best to do your homework or due diligence. My husband is a master at due diligence; he leaves no stone left unturned. He takes great pride in looking at the fine print and assessing all the potential risks, and he is valued and respected for his thoroughness. I have learned from the best, and following the example of his work ethic has served me well.

The buzzword "Due Diligence" is a reminder never to take something at face value. You are responsible for your actions; safeguard yourself by doing the groundwork, and get informed help when required to ensure you understand the outcome of your decisions. Do your "Due Diligence."

Step Up...Speak Up

It is essential to recognize and acknowledge when something is wrong, especially when it involves hatred, injustice, or the mistreatment of others. Some may say it has become commonplace and "normal" since we see it more and more in the media, on our roads, at work, in schools, and in our homes. But there is nothing *normal* about this destructive behaviour, and by doing nothing, we are effectively condoning it and allowing it to continue.

You may have heard the saying "All that is needed for evil to prevail is for good men to do nothing." As caring, conscious human beings, we have a duty to do everything in our power to speak up against evil. The buzzword "Step Up...Speak Up" is a reminder that each of us has a responsibility to ourselves and others to take positive and proactive action when needed to bring wrongful behaviour to its rightful end.

Be Grateful

Back in 1996, I learned of the book *The Simple Abundance Journal of Gratitude* by Sarah Ban Breathnach. It was the first of its kind, providing the reader with a place to record their daily moments of gratitude. I found the gratitude journal beneficial, as it helped me recognize the many blessings I did and do have in my life, unlike the magnitude of social pressures always suggesting one needs more.

Now, many years later, there are studies in the field of positive psychology. According to Harvard Health Publishing, "In positive psychology research, gratitude is strongly and consistently associated with greater happiness. Gratitude helps people feel more positive emotions, relish good experiences, improve their health, deal with adversity, and build strong relationships."[1]

In my own experience, I know this to be true, as gratitude has brought me authenticity, balance, healing, and joy. The buzzword "Be Grateful" is one to remind you to acknowledge the multitude of blessings and gifts that you presently have, all of which will enrich your life.

---

[1] Harvard Health Publishing, "Giving Thanks Can Make You Happier," updated November 22, 2011, https://www.health.harvard.edu/healthbeat/giving-thanks-can-make-you-happier.

Walk the Talk

It is always easy to talk the talk but harder to walk the walk. I have become more conscious of what I say to people, as I believe if I say it, I should mean it and do it! To me, words are only words until they are put into action. Yes, this means one must remember what one says. But that is the whole point of having a life that is authentic and true. Please don't say something unless you mean it and you are going to do it.

We all know people who like to give lip service; they love the words or the idea of something, but when it comes to following through, it does not happen. People start to remember these empty promises and take note of who are the talkers and who are the walkers. Use the buzzword "Walk the Talk" to help you stay committed, sincere, and true to your word.

Be Me

This buzzword came about with the help of a friend. I had been struggling with the challenges of acquiescing to the needs of others at a cost to myself. While sharing my angst of knowing what was right for me but being pulled in another direction because of the needs of others, my dear friend said, "Glori, just be you." A light went on, as it was so simple, and it made so much practical sense. By delving into your inner self to find your voice, your truth will always feed your authentic self.

It is said that the truth will set you free, and I have realized this to be true! I modified my wise friend's words to create the buzzword "Be Me," and I use it when I am at a crossroads and my true self is being challenged. It always realigns my thinking and reminds me to look within, to find *my* truth, which in turn sets me free.

Let Life In

In this busy and crazy world, many of us are trying to control what comes in and what goes out of our lives. At times, it feels that we are fielding many things, and when life seems to get out of control, what do we do but try to control it even more? Who are we kidding? Directing all aspects of our lives and that of others is not reality—we cannot, and we should not!

When you find that you are at your wit's end, it is time to call upon the buzzword "Let Life In." It will give you that moment to step back, breathe, and redirect your thinking to release that habitual controlling tendency and let life unfold as it will. It will provide you with a new sense of freedom and wonder because sometimes life needs to happen in its own time and way.

Find the Joy

If you have ever travelled to Europe, you might have witnessed the European philosophy of life: they "work to live," unlike in North America, where we "live to work." I will never forget visiting Italy and watching a group of Italian men taking the time to appreciate the moment; they were relaxing midday around an outdoor table, sipping coffee, and having a passionate conversation.

Seeing their collective joy, I realized their coffee breaks are much different from our coffee time here, which, in most cases, consists of rushing to line up for takeout or wait in line at a drive-through before we race to the next thing on our list. Our lives should be more than ticking boxes.

The buzzword "Find the Joy" will help direct your mind to focus on finding the pleasure, purpose, and joy in what you do and what you already have. Finding the joy in your family, home, relationships, workplace, and everywhere else in your life will enrich your body, mind, and spirit and bring you a happy and healthy life.

RELATIONSHIPS

Relationships are integral to the overall state of our body, mind, and spirit. It is important to feel a sense of belonging, be it to a family, a group of friends, a community, a workplace, and most importantly, our very selves. Communication and respect are two fundamental principles required in building the foundation of a healthy and successful relationship.

Communication, whether it be verbal, written, or the use of body language, is a means to show our commitment, dedication, and love and a way to bridge conflict, difference, and misunderstanding. Respect is vital to any healthy relationship, as it is essential to value others and be valued. For success, the needs of all must be satisfied, not just those of one individual. Hence, learning to appreciate the input of others and learning to compromise are important, as our way is not always the only way.

There are many inside and outside sources that are challenging and eroding our relationships, be it the toxic relationships that we are witnessing, our individual need to control things without regard to others, or our inability to make relationships a priority or give them the proper attention needed to be healthy and rewarding.

Each of us has the power with these *Relationships* buzzwords to direct and change our state of mind to a healthier place. They can be used internally to empower oneself or outwardly to communicate with others. They will strengthen and build your relationships positively and proactively to enrich your lives and the lives of those around you.

Dig Deeper

It was when I was hitting roadblocks with a loved one that I was at a loss on how to help our struggling relationship. I know there are many kinds of relationships, some that augment and feed us and others that challenge us. We have the choice to build positive and healthy relationships and avoid unhealthy ones.

In my case, I wanted to save this unhealthy relationship. Reading the book, *The Dance of Anger*, by Harriet Lerner, helped me refocus my energy on learning more about this loved one and their life experience. In doing so, it brought new insights into who they were and why they acted as they did.

This path brought me new understanding, patience, forgiveness, and helped me be more aware of how to navigate through this relationship. Use the buzzword "Dig Deeper" when you need to move out of a heightened emotional state and look closer at the cause and not the effect.

Be Brave

I was meeting a friend at a coffee shop to discuss some issues that were affecting our relationship. I knew things were going to be uncomfortable with what was going to be shared, but it was needed to move our relationship forward in a positive way.

My stomach was in knots as I envisioned our conversation when a passing car caught my attention; its license plate read "Be Brave." I smiled then looked to the heavens, for there was the message I needed to receive at this moment in time. It gave me the strength to realize that this conversation was needed to help mend a struggling relationship.

The buzzword "Be Brave" is one to call upon when you need the strength to do what you need to do. It will help refocus your mind on the matter at hand and not the fear of dealing with a challenging or uncomfortable situation.

Respect Difference

We are all unique individuals, and like snowflakes, no two are exactly alike! It is wonderful to see the diversity that we have in our lives, and we have the opportunity to learn and grow by celebrating differences in others.

Although we may not always understand these differences or even believe them for ourselves, we must respect them, for there are many different roads that can take us to the same destination. The buzzword "Respect Difference" helps us redirect our minds to eliminate any preconceived judgment, prejudice, or personal preference and move us forward in a new state of acceptance by celebrating differences in ourselves and others.

For the Team

In many families and relationships, people are introduced into this intimate and sacred fold, be it a new husband, wife, child, or best friend. In many cases, like a recipe, this addition changes the original flavour by augmenting and adding new spice and dimension, while at other times, it may diminish the taste and make it bitter.

Many learn to adapt, as life has many moving parts, and change is inevitable, although not always welcome. Others will fight tooth and nail to preserve that original recipe, sometimes at the cost of others and the very thing they are trying to protect! So, when you are struggling to include specific individuals at a family gathering—like your aunt who talks but does not listen, your father-in-law who is moody, or your sister's best friend who is, let's say, way too much cayenne pepper, use the buzzword "For the Team" to help you through.

This buzzword will redirect your mind to the realization that relationships are not only about us but also about *others*. So, in the case of my sister's best friend, I will take the time to be in the moment, talk, and break bread with her best friend because I love my sister, and to honour her, I will honour someone important to her. It is that simple—take one "For the Team" and for the good of the family and relationships.

Dark Cloud

When you are striving to be a good person and live a positive and proactive life, it is always a shock to come upon someone who is angry, mean-spirited, or unpleasant and even more so when they direct their negativity at you. I know it can feel personal, but some of these people just do not want to be happy and will try to darken any form of light that crosses their paths.

The buzzword "Dark Cloud" is a reminder to ignore and limit the impact of another person's negative energy. No matter what, don't let someone else affect who you are, and always let your light shine!

Stop Bullying Me

At times in our life, we may rationalize how people treat us. However, there is no reason, excuse, explanation, or justification that warrants one to bully us. The buzzword "Stop Bullying Me" directs our minds to recognize this behaviour as bullying or harassment.

We can use this buzzword out loud to defend ourselves from a bully or silently as confirmation that this behaviour is wrong and never justified. It is the first step toward finding the courage to speak up for yourself, and it will strengthen and empower you. If you witness an incident of bullying or harassment, you can use "Stop Bullying" to call the bully out and, in doing so, support the victim.

All I Have

In many ways, we are taught to believe we can be all things to all people. We are expected to be there for everyone, at their beck and call, irrespective of our own needs. I have come to realize this is not reality, as there will always be someone who has a need that cannot be filled. We are not fair to ourselves or others when we race from one thing to another, not wanting to disappoint someone or trying to please everyone. There will always be people who, no matter what you do for them, it will never be enough!

The buzzword "All I Have" is a healthy reminder to ourselves and others that we are only human, and with the limited time and energy that we have, there really is only so much we can do. It is our personal choice as to how we share our time and energy with others. Be realistic with how you share yours, and do not be afraid to say that this is "All I Have."

Not My Issue

It is fascinating to me where one can find inspiration. On one occasion, I found it in a community centre swimming pool. I had decided to do something that I had not done since my high school days: swim lengths.

While I was taking a breather, a fellow swimmer and I engaged in a conversation that led him to share with me the adapted Buddhist philosophy he follows. He said, "There are three important things in life: one, how you love; two, how gently you live your life; and three, how you let go of things that are not yours." With his wise words and joyful spirit, he inspired me! His words resonated with me, and I found the third one particularly interesting. At the time, I was working on how to "let go of things that are not yours."

To provide context, I am one who likes to be on time wherever I go. However, some people in my life are habitually late. Instead of them recognizing and accepting the problem for what it is, they try to deflect ownership by pointing the finger at me and saying that I have the issue by not being flexible. So, when you come upon those individuals who, intentionally or not, try to deflect their issues onto you, call upon the buzzword "Not My Issue" to reaffirm that this has nothing to do with you…and let it go!

Building, Not Breaking

In many challenging relationships, we struggle with communication. We get frustrated by the lack of understanding or ability to get our point across to come together. The greatest gift for a relationship is how we deal with this adversity.

We can choose positive, proactive words and actions that bridge differences, or we can break any bonds of partnership with harmful and abusive behaviour. The buzzword "Building, Not Breaking" helps direct the mind to be conscious of what message we are sending and to acknowledge we have the power to choose our words.

This Is Hurtful

I am not sure where the saying "Sticks and stones may break my bones, but names will never hurt me" came from, but they were wrong. Words can hurt, and they can degrade, demean, demoralize, discourage, disgrace, dishearten, dishonour, and discredit, and those are just the "d" words.

Once you say something, it cannot be unsaid, and you cannot fall back on the old, empty phrase "I didn't mean it" or "I was just kidding." You may think you have every right to say what you want, but you must realize that you are accountable to yourself and others when using damaging and hurtful words.

The buzzword "This Is Hurtful" is a reminder to think before you speak, text, or tweet, and if your words are harmful, then refrain from sharing them. The words you share reflect who you are as a person and can impact the lives of others.

At Arm's Length

In our lives, we interact with all types of people, some who enrich and fuel us and others who only take our energy and, in doing so, deplete us. However, when we find ourselves in relationships that consume all of our energy without giving back, it is vital to our overall health and well-being that we learn how to manage these relationships.

The buzzword "At Arm's Length" is used in those one-sided relationships that run us until empty. So, to cope, we may need to set up boundaries to keep us safe and healthy.

Pushing Rope

We all have relationships that can be challenging; maybe you are too much alike or perhaps too different. No matter, you know that your time together is going to be, let's say, "eventful." So, when innocent conversations start to become heated debates, and you know they are not listening or open to hearing your position, use the buzzword "Pushing Rope" to redirect your mind to the reality that you will be wasting your energy and it's best to agree to disagree, change topics, or if needed, gracefully remove yourself to defuse the situation.

It is always great to share new ideas and thoughts but only when you are with those who are open-minded and willing to listen and share productively. For those closed-minded people who are locked in, save your energy, as you are just "Pushing Rope."

It's Me

One day while diligently working at my desk at the office, I noticed an odd odour. Not knowing where it was coming from, I got up to investigate. I searched around my desk and down the hall. When the odour followed me, I came to the realization that it was me! The culprit being a newfound deodorant that was obviously not working.

I found it interesting that my first reaction was to look elsewhere and not at myself. So, when we are in a situation and are at odds with others, we cannot forget how we personally fit into the equation, as at times, we, in fact, are the problem. Hence, we must be conscious enough to recognize that our actions and decisions can impact others. The buzzword "It's Me" can help us take ownership and be accountable for what we do, then adjust accordingly to be positive and proactive in our relationships.

Forgive Them

It is only human for us to have expectations of others; some expectations might seem reasonable, whereas others might be a real stretch. As I continue to learn about my relationships and those of others, I have come to a new understanding that someone may not love me the way I would like, but they are loving me with everything they have.

This has helped me realize we are all trying to do the best we can with the life experiences presented to us. For some, these experiences may harden and limit people in certain aspects of their lives; for example, they might feel they are unable to trust someone again or be unable to say "sorry" or "I love you."

We must recognize these limitations, lend a hand when we can, and find forgiveness if someone cannot meet our expectations. "Forgive Them" is a buzzword that can help direct us to be gentle with others and find peace within ourselves.

PARENTING

I believe parenting to be the hardest and most rewarding job on earth, given the honour and privilege to love, nurture, and guide individuals in life. I do not have any children of my own and hence do not know firsthand the trials and tribulations of being a parent. Yet I am blessed to have nieces, nephews, and children in my life, and this experience has provided its own set of insights.

This section is not only for those who are parents and relatives but also for those outside the family circle who may be guiding forces in a child's life—caregivers, coaches, friends, mentors, neighbours, teachers, and others. These *Parenting* buzzwords were created with the hope to energize, open new forms of communication, build trust, establish boundaries, and affirm love for one another.

I Am Listening

One of my greatest indulgences is when I spend time with someone who is truly listening to me. It gives me a sense of worth that I am valued and that someone wants to hear what I have to share. The art of listening is a gift, one that is hard to find in the age of distractions, interruptions, and racing from one thing to another, but when it does happen, it is magical.

I believe some children stop talking to their parents because they are no longer heard. In my observations, some parents spend that precious time with their children teaching and preaching but often forget about the vital listening part. "I Am Listening" is a powerful buzzword, for it can bring intimacy, respect, trust, and understanding.

It is a time when you completely rid your mind of any distractions and concentrate on what your child is saying. If you are truly there, they will know it, feel it, and trust it, and they will be empowered by it. Listening creates a win-win scenario, as it gives your child the confidence to share, which strengthens them as individuals and, in doing so, strengthens your relationship.

Two-Way Street

As a baby boomer raised in the "me generation," I was fuelled by the importance of my own needs. Yes, my needs are important, but so are the needs of others.

The buzzword "Two-Way Street" is a great way to direct our minds to the reality that there are others on our path of life…and not all streets are one way. To disregard the needs and safety of others on a two-way street, we are driving dangerously and can cause frustration, road rage, or even an accident.

We must recognize this for ourselves and our children, as it is not always about "me." We must consider the needs of others, for doing so is an integral part of a healthy relationship and a fulfilling life, as the road ahead is most often a "Two-Way Street."

House Rules

Healthy households have rules to maintain fairness within a group of individuals to keep everyone happy and working well together. Rules help us develop respect for one another, and in many cases, children crave and need ground rules. Having a set of ground rules can give children a sense of comfort and stability.

As parents, if you are the one paying the bills, you deserve to lay down some rules and have them honoured and respected, so do not hesitate to set up "House Rules." Yes, there will be times that you may need to bend them, but exercise caution, as doing so may set a new precedent for everyone. Also, by saying, "Hey, it's not me, it's the House Rules," you can deflect any personal attacks and prevent a good-cop, bad-cop scenario from developing. The buzzword "House Rules" will help you set guidelines to keep your household harmonious.

Give Them Tools

Sometimes when there is a problem, we find it is easier to tell someone what to do or just do the job ourselves instead of taking the time and energy needed to give someone the guidance and tools to help them do it for themselves. When given an opportunity to teach, we need to refrain from doing the job for our children, be it doing their homework, completing a project, or paying their credit card bills. Instead, we need to help them by giving them the tools so they can do their own work, which will promote independent thinking and living. The buzzword "Give Them Tools" will redirect your mind to facilitate the giving of these tools to your children to better equip them to lead and live their own lives.

I Believe in You

I had the wonderful opportunity to work with two amazing summer students who became my Thursday lunch buddies. We would share stories about our different cultures, families, and life aspirations.

One day, I was preparing a special Canadian lunch for them, which included homemade macaroni and cheese. While trying to warm up our lunch in the faulty office toaster oven, one of the students heard my words of angst, frustration, and doubt at completing this task. He simply said, "I believe in you." And there it was, out of the mouths of babes—these simple, reassuring words that brought a smile to my face and gave me the confidence that I could achieve anything!

I loved the way that these words made me feel; they empowered me, and I knew that this was a great buzzword. When using "I Believe in You," you inspire your children without taking over or telling them what to do; instead, you give them the confidence to find their own inner strength and fortitude.

Convince Me

As children are growing and wanting to expand their responsibilities, the buzzword "Convince Me" is a great one to have in your toolbox. It puts the onus on your child to do their homework and gather the necessary information to formulate and articulate why they can handle a new responsibility or privilege. On the other hand, "Convince Me" allows you to pause and not say no or yes right away but gives you the time to decide if they are truly ready or not.

If you are not convinced, you can say so and provide them with direction on what they still need to do to get your permission. If you are convinced and say yes, then you will be allowing them to grow and experience something new. In doing so, this process will also confirm for your child that by formulating their ideas and doing the work, they can achieve their goals.

Need Your Help

Many of us fall into the superhero trap: we try to do everything for our families—tending to every individual need, maintaining a home, and working a full-time job. Oh yes, not only do we strive to do everything, but we also expect to excel at each one of them! It is not humanly possible to live this way, as it does not serve ourselves or those around us well.

The time has come to start sharing responsibilities by introducing the buzzword "Need Your Help" as a means to help children learn the reality of what it takes to run a family and household and maintain a career. This buzzword teaches them that we all have limitations and that needing help from others is normal and human.

By trying to do everything, we forget how wonderful it is to feel needed, and by reaching out, we are giving those around us the gift of being needed. It will build their confidence and help define a family that works in partnership. So be a real superhero, and introduce the buzzword "Need Your Help" into your family life, and watch how your relationships and those around you grow, prosper, and thrive.

Let Them Lead

I believe the greatest gift a parent can give their child is helping them find their own voice. Yes, it is easy to point children in the direction that we believe is best for them, but the time comes when this does not always bring about independent thinking or allow them to find their unique paths in life.

The buzzword "Let Them Lead" redirects your mindset to the realization that your children must formulate their own thoughts, ideas, desires, and wishes, which allows them to take the lead role in their lives. It is vital for their growth, especially at a time when there are so many voices telling them what to do, say, think, and wear. They need to dig deep, go within, and find their own voices. In allowing them to do so, you will help them find the personal fulfillment needed for a balanced and healthy life. We can help them if we "Let Them Lead."

Store Is Closed

Some stores are open 24/7 these days, so this concept might be hard to grasp, but it is an important one, as some children feel that they can ask for anything at any time and it just materializes. We are not serving children well in this regard. Giving them everything they desire without work or patience, and often without any gratitude in return, only brings about entitlement and wanting more. "Store Is Closed" is a practical buzzword to help establish boundaries and expectations and to teach children that, in life, there are many times when there is just no more!

Teaching Moment

As children find their way in life, there will be times when their choices may disappoint, enrage, sadden, or shock you. Unfortunately, these events are part of life.

It is in these moments that one has the opportunity to teach children and help them learn and grow from a challenging decision or a mistake they have made. What makes these moments essential is that you are there to help guide, direct, support, and love them through it! As parents, you have greater knowledge and insight than your children, and it is your responsibility to help build and inspire them to be the best they can be.

The buzzword "Teaching Moment" is one to use when an opportunity—be it good, bad, or ugly—presents itself. Celebrate this moment as an opportunity to prepare your child with new life skills that will help them succeed. Parents should not try to raise perfect children but conscientious children—those who know right from wrong, take responsibility for their choices, and learn from their decisions.

Love Them More

There are times when one may see a child's negative behaviour and become perplexed trying to figure out where the behaviour is coming from and why. At times like these, we need to look back to when we were their age and recall when we were struggling to find our voice or our purpose or just trying to belong.

The world has changed, and it is even harder to navigate, with its negative forces trying to draw in the innocent and vulnerable. When emotions and anxiety are running high, use the buzzword "Love Them More" to look beyond the hurtful and mean-spirited rage and see the fragile and frightened child behind it.

CHILDREN

As adults, mentors, and role models in a child's life, we play an important part in the development of the younger generation. These are challenging times, and forces beyond our control are pushing and pulling our children. With all that they are facing in their young and innocent lives, they will need some assistance in finding the tools to navigate these turbulent waters.

We have a valuable opportunity to introduce them to the power of buzzwords and how they can benefit from using them. These *Children* buzzwords will help our young ones develop the skill of using their state of mind to enrich, empower, and prepare for this ever-changing world.

Be the Best Me

Every day we have the opportunity to be our best selves. We know what is right and what's wrong. We know when we are kind to ourselves and others, and we know when we are mean-spirited. This knowledge comes from what we say, what we think, what we write, and the energy we release, be it positive or negative. Know that all of this affects us to the core.

I believe that the positive energy we send out to the world fills us to the brim with good and wonderful feelings and feeds us in a healthy way. The opposite is also true. If we choose to send out negative energy, it will grow within us and poison our body and mind and those around us. You can find negative energy anywhere, but it is *your* choice how you live your life and what you want to feed to your body and mind…so choose positive!

When you wake up every morning, say the buzzword "Be the Best Me" to help direct your mind to be the best you. In the evening, think about how you succeeded that day and how you can be even better tomorrow. Continuing this every day will make you stronger, happier, and more fulfilled by being positive and your best self. You will find, when you share your light, love, and positive energy, it will be the greatest gift to yourself and others.

I Am Loved

I want you to do something very, very important. Take your right hand and reach across your body, place it on your left shoulder, and hold it there. Now take your left hand and reach across your body, place it on your right shoulder, and hold it there. Great, now squeeze and give yourself a loving hug! Yes, I know this might seem silly, but trust me, it is not.

It is essential that people feel a sense of love for oneself, and the buzzword "I Am Loved" is perfect. It is important to understand that you are a unique and special person. So, wrap your arms and mind around the buzzword "I Am Loved," and do just that; love the person you are. If you are not feeling the love at this moment, well, get to it; direct your mind and life around the many things and people you love, and love you for you.

Not My Thing

As we journey through life, we try many different things and gravitate toward what we enjoy and feel confident doing. We also learn along the way that being human means we may not be good at everything we try. For those things we no longer enjoy nor want to spend time and energy doing, or we simply are not good at, recognize this reality and use the buzzword "Not My Thing" to let go of those things you do not enjoy.

This buzzword can also help when someone tries to pressure you into something you do not want to do. By using "Not My Thing," you allow others to know where you stand. It is empowering to have a sense of self and to discover who you are, what you are all about, and what direction you want your life to take.

Journal

There was a time in my life when I thought no one understood me. Hey, that was probably true because I did not understand myself either. Different voices were telling me what to do, say, wear, and above all, how to live. They were so loud I could not hear my own voice. I needed to find my voice to find my own life, so I did something that helped: I started to journal.

I put pen to paper and shared my inner thoughts, fears, troubling events, achievements, dreams, life questions, and anything else I wanted to unload. There were times I was so mad I could not write fast enough, and there were times I was so sad that my writing would bring me to tears; it would inspire me and, at other times, make me laugh. The more I wrote, the more I learned why I was feeling the way I was, which helped me understand me!

Journaling provided a safe place for me without interference or judgment, and it allowed me to gather my thoughts and reach out to others for help. So, when your life is a whirlwind of emotions or you're trying to understand a specific problem or looking for direction in your life, call upon the buzzword "Journal" and find a quiet place and do just that: journal! It is a gift to yourself.

Only One Chapter

I remember, when I was younger, there were moments that I thought would define or label me and possibly ruin my life—be it something unexpected, something embarrassing, something I did not understand, something hurtful, something stupid, or something that I could not control and felt that I would be ashamed of for the rest of my life. I wish someone had been there to reassure me that I would not ruin my life because of one chapter.

Let me be that person who tells you there will be some chapters in your life that will make you so happy you will not be able to stop smiling, laughing, and singing. And yes, others will be so hard and painful, you might need to cry yourself to sleep or scream with rage. But know that each and every chapter is needed to help build, inspire, and strengthen the person that you are.

Trust me when I say the buzzword "Only One Chapter" is a reminder that your life will be a multitude of different chapters. If your current one is hard and painful, there will be another one that will bring you great happiness and joy!

Think of Others

I have a simple question to see if you are mindful of others. If you are the one to use the last of the toilet paper, do you always replace the roll for the next person, or do you do nothing and leave the next person, literally, with their pants down? Unless you are going to move to a desert island and live the rest of your life alone, it is important to be aware of and include the needs of others in your life.

To be a conscientious and caring human being, you must "Think of Others." So, when you use the last of the toilet paper, "Think of Others" and replace the roll. When you use the last of the bread, "Think of Others" and tell someone or add it to the shopping list. When you're with friends and you are the only one talking, "Think of Others" and let someone else share what is going on in their life.

Once you start using this buzzword, it will become a habit and a part of who you are as a person. Your life and the lives of others will be richer for it.

Ouch, That Hurt

OK, I know this sounds light, but it is meant to be simple and to the point. Think about when you are with your friends, and one of them says something that hurts you, and you just let it pass, but their comment continues to fester inside you.

In using the buzzword "Ouch, That Hurt" it makes the other person know that they have crossed the line and have caused you pain. It will allow them to understand you better as you set boundaries with open communication, which is needed to maintain a healthy relationship. This buzzword helps everyone, as there are times when others may not know they have hurt you, and it is important that you let them know when they do.

Not Right

I believe our bodies are amazing, with built-in warning signs that tell us when something feels "Not Right." It could be a knot in our stomach, or when something is troubling us and we keep thinking about it over and over.

It's not always easy to look at something head-on when it makes us uncomfortable or if it means making a difficult decision, but doing so is necessary for the health of our body, mind, and spirit. Even if you try to ignore it, your body will not let go of this feeling until you do something. This buzzword is one to use to acknowledge your feeling that something is "Not Right" and give you the confidence and strength to act on it.

Free to Be Me

In this world of social media, where we can see everyone's life, it is sometimes hard to figure out where we fit. Yes, it is easier to follow along and copy what everyone else is doing, saying, or wearing, but this may not be you.

The buzzword "Free to Be Me" is a reminder that you have the power and choice to be a unique individual. Don't look to the lives of others to find what is your truth; look deep within yourself, for the truth is there waiting to be discovered. Look to what inspires you, challenges you, and feeds you, and honour those things. Although it might be different from others, be courageous and true to yourself by using the buzzword "Free to Be Me" to reaffirm that you have the right to be the unique individual you are!

HEALTH

Our health and well-being are vital elements for a happy and fulfilling life. For us to flourish, we must do everything we can to nurture our bodies—a most precious gift. We have seen many advancements in financial wealth, technology, and other areas; however, we are lagging in our overall personal health.

We have the power to change and reinstate our health as a top priority in our lives. These *Health* buzzwords will help you redirect your state of mind to succeed in this lifesaving area.

Honour Thy Body

We only get one body in a lifetime. When we are young, we think we are invincible and that the choices we make will not have any impact, but we are wrong. Everything we do affects this intricate vessel we call our body. We need to appreciate all it can do and find the balance and harmony that is important to our daily living.

Our bodies are amazing, but there comes a time when they struggle with the available 24/7 social media, long working hours and related stress, and the lack of regular, nutritious food and much-needed rest to recuperate. We are pushing our bodies past their limits, which will invariably create problems. The buzzword "Honour Thy Body" is a reminder that we need to respect and nurture our bodies, and by living within those limits, we will bring balance and harmony to our lives.

Trust Mother Nature

My philosophy has always been if I cannot read or pronounce the ingredients on a label, then there is a high probability my body will not know what to do with it or how to digest it, if it even can. Our food has become overcomplicated, almost as if we think we can make things better than Mother Nature. Well, that is not the case!

I cannot tell you how many times I've read how something has been improved: "this" is better than "that," then read "that" is now better than "this." I always choose good old natural food, which has not been modified or recreated. So, when you feel you are being pulled in one direction then in another by the latest news cycle, use the buzzword "Trust Mother Nature," as it will help direct you to where you *naturally* need to go.

Fix What's Broken

Much like a warning light in a car telling us that something is wrong, pain is our body's warning light. When we are feeling pain, our bodies are screaming, "Help me!"

I have come to believe that much of our health care industry's focus is on alleviating pain; however, many times, alleviating pain only serves as a temporary solution. By not addressing the underlying cause of pain, we enter a perpetual cycle of treating the symptom and not the actual problem. When it comes to our health, the buzzword "Fix What's Broken" is a reminder to direct your mind to the root cause of the problem and spend your time, energy, and money in this area, as this will prove to be most beneficial and valuable to you.

Eat Right

I am genuinely amazed by the intricacy of the human body and how everything is uniquely connected to achieve success. Our bodies do not ask much of us, other than to be nourished and to get rest—and oh yes, to listen to it when something is wrong.

I came to a new appreciation and understanding of my body after I read the book *Eat Right 4 Your Type* by Dr. Peter J. D'Adamo. I learned that our bodies, as unique as they are, have recommended dietary and lifestyle choices based on our blood type, that being O, A, B, or AB. Each blood type, being our internal chemistry, reacts differently to the food we eat, and by introducing the recommended foods for our blood type, we can improve our overall health.

This knowledge has given me a new respect for my body and has empowered me to know that I can change my state of health by the food I eat. So, for those looking to achieve optimum health, consider changing your food choices to match your blood type and call upon the buzzword "Eat Right" to help you on your journey.

Quality, Not Quantity

Our world is changing in many areas, especially when it comes to food. Portion sizes are getting larger to rationalize increasing food prices, while the nutritional value is getting smaller to almost non-existent. We are learning that what tastes good does not necessarily mean it is good for us, as some food is not "real" at all. Food can be overprocessed with additives and flavour enhancers and, in some cases, are chemically created…yikes!

It should not be surprising that our bodies are undernourished, damaged, and failing when there is no natural nutritional value in food that is not real. So, it is up to us to find the truth about what we are eating and what it is that is fuelling our bodies. We must remember, we need real food to keep our bodies nutritionally fed, fuelled, and functioning. The buzzword "Quality, Not Quantity" directs our attention to the quality of food we eat.

Food, Not Filler

I come from a family of cheese-and-cracker eaters, who will defend this as a meal. This dynamic has led us to many great debates, which have left me starving, literally and figuratively.

No matter what team you are on, we must be mindful that our bodies need to eat real food packed with nutrients, not only fillers. Our bodies are amazing in every way, and they need to be fed and fuelled, much like a high-performance car. If you are going to drive it, you must fuel it with premium-grade fuel to get maximum performance.

The buzzword "Food, Not Filler" will help remind you that although you may have fillers and snacks within your day, you must have sufficient nutritious food for your body. A car without the proper fuel will suffer from engine trouble and start to break down. Don't end up like the broken-down car; feed your body like it's a high-performance machine.

Breathe One, Two, Three

We know that we cannot live without food or water, but let's not forget that oxygen is our first and foremost necessity for survival. New evidence suggests that proper breathing is even more important than we have generally come to know. These findings are outlined in more detail in the book *Breath: The New Science of a Lost Art* by James Nestor. His research includes looking to past civilizations and their cultures and practices, interviewing specialists in related areas, and conducting his very own experiment of nose breathing versus mouth breathing.

What I have come to learn is that proper breathing is essential for our body's day-to-day health and well-being and can be a built-in stress reliever. So, in times of anxiety, anger, fear, or when you need a sense of calm, use the buzzword "Breathe One, Two, Three." It will direct your mind to concentrate on inhaling deeply to a count of three then slowly exhaling through a pursed-lip mouth. It will help rebalance your body and state of mind.

I'm a Cadillac

A very dear friend of mine was sharing with me the experience she had with her doctor. When discussing her upcoming surgery and optional medical treatments, she asked the doctor whether her age—a young seventy-eight—would have any impact on the outcome. He paused, looked up from her medical records, and said, "You're a Cadillac."

These words made my friend laugh and, in turn, bolstered her confidence about the health of her body. I told her she just found her buzzword, "I'm a Cadillac," and to use it throughout her surgery and recovery. This buzzword was perfect for her, and I share it with you, as it can inspire and strengthen your state of mind, giving you the confidence to move forward, as you, too, should see yourself as a Cadillac.

Fill Me with Light

We have the power to feed our bodies in any way we choose; this also means the energy that we infuse into our minds, be it positive or negative. I believe it is essential for our health and well-being that we bring light, love, and positive energy into our bodies to dissolve the negative energy that may be a result of what is transpiring around us or within us.

This light can encompass anything that generates a positive feeling within us, be it sitting in a sun-filled room, a gentle walk, a quiet meditation, or something that brings a sense of peace or joy. Whether it be real or through visualization, the buzzword "Fill Me with Light" is meant to direct your mind to the knowledge that you have the power to change your mental and physical state by feeding yourself in this positive way.

SPIRITUAL

Spirituality means different things to different people, as there are many different beliefs, practices, and religions in this world. I believe there are many roads to the same destination, especially so when we are each trying to find a sense of belonging through our community, our generosity of spirit, and most importantly, love.

In this section, I refer to God and the Father, but in doing so, that does not exclude all the other divine, positive powers of the Universe that people hold close to their heart. May these *Spiritual* buzzwords help you recognize and celebrate the light within and share it to bring unity and love to others.

Honour Thyself

We have been blessed and honoured with life. Many of us do not truly realize that we are intricate and amazing individuals and that this gift of life must be cherished. The body, mind, and spirit need to be united and working in harmony to accomplish all that we are destined to do. We are the guardians of this vessel, and it is up to us to nurture, respect, and most of all, honour it.

It has been said, "Your body is your temple." The buzzword "Honour Thyself" is a reminder that you need to be mindful of this complex and magnificent being that you are and care for it in a positive, loving way.

God's Plan

There is a wonderful saying that goes like this: "If you want to make God laugh, just make a plan." I have always liked this saying because it puts life into perspective.

As much as we think we can make plans and control our lives and the world, this is truly not a realistic belief. We will always be confronted with surprises and unforeseen circumstances that will impact our plans. As a result, we tend to focus our energy on things that did not happen instead of trusting that when one door closes, it allows for others to open.

"God's Plan" is a buzzword to help us loosen our hold on life and the perception that we can control everything. It is time to let life happen, for there is a greater plan in place: "God's Plan."

Rejoice Always

It was by chance, providence, or divine intervention that I came across an interview with Mary C. Neal while she was on *The Today Show*. She was sharing her story of a kayaking accident that changed her life in more ways than she could imagine.

In her book *7 Lessons from Heaven*, she provides a detailed account of her physical drowning, her entering heaven's doors, and all that she came to learn from her visit with God. With everything she endured, it was during her recovery in the hospital that she turned to the Bible and found these words: "Rejoice Always" (1 Thessalonians 5:16).

These words, and the message they carried, became an essential part of her state of mind and helped lead her to a successful and miraculous recovery. Let the buzzword "Rejoice Always" be one to inspire you to give thanks and celebrate your life, no matter your current state of being.

Feed Your Soul

There are a lot of dark things happening in our world at this time. With technology at our fingertips, we have immediate access to every devastating and sad event that takes place.

We need to find balance in our lives and add that much-needed light and positive energy to outweigh the dark and negative, be it through nature, inspirational writings, scriptures, gentle music, joyful conversation, or whatever grounds us and brings peace and balance to our lives. The buzzword "Feed Your Soul" will help redirect you to the positive influences you need daily to keep your body, mind, and spirit healthy.

God Wink

I was reading Oprah Winfrey's book *What I Know for Sure*, where she introduced me to the concept of a "God wink"—thank you, Oprah! I never gave it much thought but then realized I had these in my life.

One occurred many years ago when I was involved in the entertainment business. As anyone in "the biz" knows, the industry can fixate on perfection, and at the time, I was trying to perfect my teeth and smile. I had just spent an exorbitant amount of money and time on this obsession, and I was still unhappy. I felt my imperfect teeth would be my failing.

At my part-time job as a receptionist, a client was waiting at the elevator. I pulled my attention from my angst and heartache to say goodbye and wish him a nice day. The gentleman paused then said, "You have the most beautiful smile!" Well, there it was, a God wink! A gentle reminder to me that a beautiful smile is not about perfect teeth. The buzzword "God Wink" is one to call upon when you witness this blessing, this affirmation, this gift from God, and with it, know that God is with you on your life journey.

I Am Blessed

Something powerful happens when we feed ourselves with positive affirmations. It is easy to take things for granted and forget to look at the many blessings we have in our lives—a beautiful sunrise, a squirrel manoeuvring in a tree, a neighbour's friendly wave, a stranger who lets you in on the highway, a warm house to which you come home.

No matter how large or small, give thanks for these bountiful blessings that surround you each day. Use the buzzword "I Am Blessed" to help direct your mind to the blessings that are presently in your life and feeding your body, mind, and spirit.

Stretch Me

Over one Thanksgiving weekend, I attended a church service while travelling, where I was welcomed with open arms by their minister and congregation. During the service, the minister shared that we should give thanks to our family and friends, even to those who "stretch" us. I loved it! His words made me, and the rest of the congregation, laugh; it was a fascinating message.

It was a great reminder that, yes, we will always have those relationships that challenge us. Instead of seeing them as negative or being a problem, we can turn that thought around and see the relationship as an opportunity for growth. Hence, this fabulous buzzword, "Stretch Me," was born, and in extremely challenging times, I expand it to "Stretch, Baby, Stretch."

In God's Hands

Many things in life are not in our control, and we must learn that it is not our responsibility to carry the weight of the world on our shoulders. We are not alone, for God is there for every one of us. As we are only human, there will be times when the best we do for ourselves and others is not enough.

When we feel that we can do no more, we must shift this burden from our troubled mind and soul and place it with God. The buzzword "In God's Hands" is a reminder that He walks with us each step of the way, and there will be times when He alone will carry the load for us.

Here I Am, Lord

When I first heard the hymn "Here I Am, Lord" by Dan Schutte, it brought me to tears. The beautiful music and touching lyrics moved my soul. This song spoke to me and opened me up to a whole new way of thinking and living. I am one of God's children. We are all God's children, and we are here on this earth to be of service to others.

We each have unique gifts, and it is our responsibility to find, hone, and share them. Your gift may be providing loving parental guidance, having a dedicated work ethic as a paid employee or volunteer, helping and teaching those in need, or simply being kind to others. No matter what your gift, by sharing it to bring light, love, and positive energy, you are serving God. The buzzword "Here I Am, Lord" is to remind you to open your heart and soul and hear what God is asking you to give of yourself to others.

Angel on Earth

We have angels here on earth. We meet them throughout our lives, some of whom remain with us, while others only stay for a brief time. We must recognize these angels and honour them, for they are gifts from God. However, this goes even further. What if we were the angel? Would it change the way we live? Would we treat people with more kindness? Would we love with a more open heart? Would we direct our lives more purposefully? The buzzword "Angel on Earth" is to help direct you to celebrate those who touch you in this unique and sacred way, and to share the angel within you.

Keep the Faith

There will always be rocky roads on our journeys and ones that will take energy, patience, and time to manoeuvre. Some will be easier than others, but when you find that you are stopped in your tracks and don't know what direction to take, call upon the buzzword "Keep the Faith." It will help direct you to stay focused, trust the path that you have chosen, and be reassured you are not alone in your life journey, for God is with you always.

My Purpose

I have this beautiful image of meeting our heavenly Father when my days here on earth have come to an end. His arms will open lovingly to embrace me, and He will say, "My child, what did you share of yourself on earth?" To me, this question is a gentle reminder that we each have a purpose in life, and what we share of ourselves touches the world.

Even in darkness, we must find the strength and fortitude to continue to shine our light. The buzzword "My Purpose" is to help direct your mind to your path in life that honours the gifts you have been blessed with and, more importantly, to empower you to share them with others.

WORKPLACE

Our workplace environment plays a vital role in our health and well-being, particularly given the amount of time we invest in our jobs. This environment has changed dramatically over the years due to the lightning speed of technology, an increase in demands, a decrease in employees, and at times, the unrealistic expectations of the business world itself. The bottom line is the top priority at all costs, even if that cost is you.

At times, you are managing not only your day-to-day workload but also the complex relationships within the office. All of this is taxing on your physical and mental state, and you must recognize that the real priority in your working life is you! It is important to your overall health and well-being to find the time to take a break, rest your body and mind, refuel, and find a way to cope with toxic behaviours. Yes, I know that many will say this is not possible, but if you want to remain healthy, you must make it happen. The following *Workplace* buzzwords will help you direct your mind to find the balance needed to honour not only your job but also yourself!

Read the Signs

When we are entering into a new job opportunity, it is not just the job itself that we need to assess but also the other elements of the company. The position might be the greatest one in the world; however, is positive leadership evident? Do they walk the walk? Are there signs of bullying? Does the company respect and value their employees? Are the employees happy? When we are working as long and as hard as we do, our work environment must be a positive and healthy one.

The buzzword "Read the Signs" directs you to take note of the many things that help determine if a work environment is right for you. To grow and thrive in the workplace, you need to be respected and valued, so don't waste your time and talent if the workplace is dysfunctional, toxic, and unhealthy. Life is too short, and the stress of staying in this kind of environment will only cut your life even shorter! You deserve better, so find a company that values you as much as you value them.

Take the Initiative

A wonderful job opportunity came my way. Although outside my comfort zone with the role and responsibilities, I was told that my strengths were valued and that on-the-job training would teach me the skills I was lacking. Early on, I realized that shortcuts were the teaching preference instead of the full set of tools needed for the job. My supervisor would go on to tell me I asked too many questions—hey, that's what happens when you're trying to learn and understand!

All to say, when I saw that what I needed was not being offered, it was in my power to find the tools elsewhere. The buzzword "Take the Initiative" directs you to be self-sufficient in finding proper resources to keep you at the top of your game without depending solely on others.

Head in the Game

We have been both blessed and cursed with technology and how it affects our lives, especially in the workplace. We receive a multitude of personal emails, texts, and social media notifications during the day, which results in a massive distraction from our work.

We may boast about our ability to be successful multitaskers, but research suggests it is not possible to split our brainpower. We think we are multitasking, but in fact, we are only switching back and forth between tasks, much like a pinball machine. The bumpers are the tasks, and the ball is our brain bouncing from one to the other, with each job not getting our full attention.

The buzzword "Head in the Game" is to help you focus on one thing, allowing your brain to work at its optimum. Hence, when you are at work, be at work. Your boss and co-workers will appreciate it, and your brain will love you for it.

Absolutely

I remember struggling with an issue and reluctantly asking for help. The response I received was a simple "Absolutely." It was the first time I heard this word used in this context. It was magic to my ears, and a wave of relief came over me.

I knew in that instant this would become a regular buzzword in my life, for I loved the way it made me feel and believed others would feel the same way. In the workplace, part of our job is to assist, be it our co-workers, clients, or others. Using the buzzword "Absolutely" is a great way to bring a feeling of partnership or team spirit and provides the affirmation that you will be there for them without question.

Need to Fuel

In our fast-paced work environments, we might find it hard to take a moment to breathe. There is an expectation that while you are working on today's deadline, you are also finalizing changes to yesterday's documentation, all the while keeping an eye out for the needs of tomorrow. It can become daunting, overwhelming, and at times, impossible.

While the main objective is the completion of this work, you need to remember the only person looking after your well-being is you. So, when you are at your limit or breaking point, use the buzzword "Need to Fuel" to redirect your mind to take a much-needed break or to feed that amazing body that has been working nonstop.

Great Work

Every one of us likes to be valued and appreciated for what we do on the job. It doesn't matter what role we hold, be it the boss, executive assistant, support staff, receptionist, or any other position; it takes a village to achieve success. When we feel that we've made a difference, our confidence and our self-worth are strengthened.

When someone goes out of their way to acknowledge your work, an interesting phenomenon happens: you want to work harder for them. The buzzword "Great Work" is one to use regularly to inspire your team.

Not Appropriate

There will always be those in the office environment who will push the envelope with inappropriate behaviour. Some of these people knowingly do this just to push people's buttons; the others, well, they are just clueless! It is hard to know what to do when you are put in this position, for when you say nothing, it can appear you are condoning this behaviour.

In my experience, the buzzword "Not Appropriate" works perfectly, as it sends two messages. First, it tells this person they have crossed the line, and second, it lets others know that you are not a willing participant in negative and demeaning behaviour. By speaking up, you also encourage others to do the same, which leads to a healthier working environment.

Don't Sell Out

Our business world has become a crazy one, where the focus is all about profits for the corporation and its shareholders. One can see that the company is thriving—it's bringing in huge profits; however, the mandate is to make more.

When a company is so intent on making profits at all costs, employees might find themselves pushed and prodded to cross lines. If this occurs, use the buzzword "Don't Sell Out," as it will help direct you to stay true to your convictions, values, professional reputation, and integrity. Do not let anyone or anything jeopardize your principles; at the end of the day, all you have is your reputation.

Red Flag

I had a great job opportunity where I had the luxury to work in a position for two months before being hired full-time. There were dysfunctional issues within the department, and I knew this from the start. In my mind, I thought I could help change the situation and provide a workable solution. I should point out that, at the time, I had not created or implemented my "Red Flag" buzzword. I believe if I had, it would have helped me with my initial decision process.

By identifying something as a "Red Flag," it helps you step out of a situation and see something for what it truly is before proceeding further. In my case, there were red flags—the managing administrator saying "there are no words" and, true to her word, offering no communication in challenging times; the director stating he wanted to "raise the bar," yet he was a bully who verbally abused, demeaned, and devalued his team regularly. Yes, in life, there will always be dangers and many red flags, so one needs to pay close attention to them and see them as warning signs.

Money Isn't Everything

OK, I know money is essential to our lives, be it to house, clothe, and feed us, but we have moved into a new world of wanting an excessive amount of money. Hey, how much extra money do we need? This desire for more money, in many cases, is driving us to lose our inner compass by making work our main priority. At the end of the day, it will not be a bulging bank account that will fulfill us.

We pay a high price for our blind obsession to attain more, focusing solely on the future without living in the present, with the cost being our health, families, and relationships. In doing so, we undermine our real goal of living a balanced and fulfilling life. This buzzword is a simple reminder for all of us that "Money Isn't Everything."

BUZZWORD TOOLBOX

The following buzzwords are additional ones you can include in your toolbox. Some may appear obvious; however, they are simply not used often enough. Use these buzzwords to help you build relationships, establish boundaries, and even defuse tense situations. I encourage you to use these buzzwords or create your own, which will help you be the best version of yourself and empower you on your life journey.

I Love You

These words, "I Love You," are words that all of us need to hear. Many will say, "Oh, they already know," or "I don't need to say it," but you do. These words feed the heart and soul, make one feel special and treasured, and strengthen the bond of your relationship.

I Am Sorry

It is essential in all relationships that when we recognize we've made a mistake or hurt someone, we admit it and say "I Am Sorry." These words are powerful, so use them to build a bridge, mend a heart, or right a wrong. We are all human, and we will all make mistakes at one time or another.

Thank You

It is funny how two of the simplest words, "Thank You," have been forgotten in this day and age. Yes, they are part of having good manners, but they are more than that; they show appreciation and that one's energy, time, and thoughtfulness are acknowledged and valued.

You Are Not Alone

These words are powerful in letting someone know that they are not alone on their life journey. So, when someone is facing challenging or stressful times, the buzzword "You Are Not Alone" is one to use to show a sign of support and to give someone the confidence to know that help is available to weather any storm.

It's Important to Me

Our lives are busy with the many responsibilities that are pulling us in all directions. At times, it is hard to communicate our real needs to each other, and sometimes we need more clarity. The buzzword "It's Important to Me" can be used to express that this ask is something different and especially meaningful to you with the hope that it will be honoured and respected.

Agree to Disagree

This buzzword is an oldie but truly a goodie! Sometimes in relationships, we simply are on opposite ends of the playing field. No matter what you do, you just feel differently, and no matter how much time you spend trying to convince the other that the grass is greener on your side, it's time to throw in the towel and just "Agree to Disagree."

Don't Burn Bridges

There are times in our personal or business worlds where unexpected changes occur, be it a friend's new significant other, a new employee, or the promotion of a co-worker who does not fit the role. No matter what comes about, it is important to be diplomatic and professional and to refrain from gossip and speaking negatively or disparagingly about that person. The buzzword "Don't Burn Bridges" reminds you to only speak well of people, for it defines you as a respectful individual, and one never knows how your paths will cross in the future.

Loud and Clear

When receiving direction or information that has been repeated over and over again, use the buzzword "Loud and Clear" to communicate that you have heard the message and have taken it in.

Gut Instinct

There are those who instinctively listen to a gut feeling, believing it to be intuition, a sixth sense, or nature's way of helping us in our decision-making. The buzzword "Gut Instinct" is an important one, as it will remind you to take notice, listen, respect, and value what your gut is telling you.

Line in the Sand

There are times we know we can go no further, as we feel we have compromised as much as we can. The buzzword "Line in the Sand" communicates that you have limits and boundaries need to be honoured.

Stop

Yes, the good old stop sign. I think we learned this one in kindergarten. There are times when words can inflame, aggravate, and cross lines, and when you do not have the words or energy, you can always use this buzzword or the universal hand gesture. Everyone knows what it means, and hopefully, when heard or seen, it will communicate to the other party to do just that: STOP!

Not Built That Way

This buzzword is a great way to remind each other that you are different, plain and simple. You have different thoughts, ideas, needs, and sometimes different ways of doing and processing things. The buzzword "Not Built That Way" reminds one to stop pushing for change and respect the difference.

Pushing My Button

In all relationships, there will be times when someone is going to drive you crazy. They may not know it, or they do and just enjoy doing it! The buzzword "Pushing My Button" allows you to give some warning that you are at your limit and that it's best to lay off before something blows.

Excuse Me?

Over time it is easy to get into a habit of negative dialogue. Many will call this "attitude," and it is heard in one's voice and seen in one's body language. The buzzword "Excuse Me?" is a request for a do-over, which indicates that what was shared is not acceptable and that one needs to express themselves in a different and more respectful way.

Please Let Me Speak

We all need to be heard. It is essential to the development and respect for one's voice that each of us gets an opportunity to share our ideas and thoughts. It is not always easy when you are in the heat of the moment, but the buzzword "Please Let Me Speak" can be used as a reminder that everyone has a right to be heard.

Peace

The buzzword "Peace," be it spoken or signalled by using the universal physical hand sign, always helps when things are getting off the rails, there is a misunderstanding, or no one is listening. This buzzword can provide a pause and help defuse a negative interaction.

Be Here

With the many distractions in our day, the buzzword "Be Here" is to remind you that you need to be in the present moment. If you are doing something else, you cannot be truly in the here and now. One of the greatest gifts in a relationship is someone's time, so give them the respect they deserve and "Be Here." This means turn off all technology, set aside other distractions, and give 100 percent of yourself.

You're Awesome

When someone expresses accolades for something we have done, it confirms our accomplishment and builds confidence to continue to do great things. Everyone wants to feel that they are awesome, so when they do something special, use this buzzword and tell them, "You're Awesome!"

ACKNOWLEDGMENTS

As the saying goes, "It takes a village…"

I want to take this opportunity to thank the multitude of people, relationships, and resulting experiences that have touched my life. I celebrate the good, the bad, and yes, even the ugly, for each one has helped me become who I am today: the good for inspiring me, the bad for strengthening me, and the ugly for teaching me right from wrong. It is through these vast experiences that I have learned, observed, and lived many magnificent moments as well as difficult and painful ones. Thank you to the many people who knowingly and unknowingly inspired my buzzwords and, in turn, inspired the creation of this book.

As many leave the best to last, I will do the reverse and start with the best. My dear Frank, thank you for your abundant and steadfast love and support. I honestly would not be me if you were not you, for you have always given me the freedom, respect, and understanding needed to help me accomplish my dreams. With each new creative idea, when many would ask "why," you were always there to say "when," and then help me make it happen. Thank you for believing in me and helping me grow and strive to be the best *me*, which in turn has allowed me to share my gifts. It is said that life is about the journey, and what a journey! I will always hold a special memory of us together, fireplace ablaze, and going through the first round of editing on this book. Your patience, kindness, and attention to detail have been heaven-sent. Thank you for being you and allowing me to be me. I love you.

With the mention of heaven-sent, I share a special heartfelt thank-you to my departed loved ones. Although many have been looking down from the heavens for a long time, I have always felt your love, and you have inspired me throughout my life. You are all in my heart and will always remain with me.

To my dear family and friends, thank you for being a part of my life and loving me in your own special ways. You are truly loved and treasured. Thank you for your support and for sharing an interest in my many creative projects. It seems I have been working on some of them for years, and finally, I can say this one is complete! Thank you for being there to listen, to cheer me on, and for understanding when I need to disappear and go "off the grid," giving me the space to focus and create; as you know, this is essential for me, being one who cannot walk and chew gum at the same time.

My treasured Lynnie, thank you for being a true inspiration with your courage and strength. Thank you for allowing me to share a part of your story, which I believe will help others.

At the early stages of writing this book, I attended a seminar called *The Power of the Pen*, given by graphologist Elaine Charal. Thank you, Elaine, for coming into my life for that brief moment in time. Our meeting was timely, and you empowered me more than you know to better understand myself and, in doing so, inspired me to celebrate and share these special parts of myself.

Only a writer knows how important their working environment is, and so a multitude of thanks to my dear friends Penny and John. Thank you for the opportunity to use your beautiful Toronto waterfront oasis while you were traveling the world. As I sat working at your lovely dining table, looking out over the magnificent view of open space and tranquil water, it provided the perfect setting to be creative and productive.

While in the final stages of writing this book, I had the joyful occasion to meet Simran and Sajan. Thank you both for our summer Thursday lunches together, where I had the opportunity to learn about your culture, your families, and the extraordinary individuals that you are. Your generosity of heart and spirit will be long remembered. Thank you for your interest, contributions, and encouragement to finish this book.

Thank you, Jennifer Kepler, for your amazing editing work. As stated on your website, www.cypressediting.com, "There's nothing to fear when your book is in the right hands." It was with great relief to find your quote to be true, for *the right hands*...were your hands. You not only shared your expertise with the written word and suggested ideas to make my manuscript stronger, but you also honoured me by maintaining my voice, style, and message. Thank you from the bottom of my heart—you are a gift! Also, thank you for recommending professional proofreader Amanda Kruse, as the final set of eyes on my book. Thank you, Amanda, for your great work! And thank you Jason Anderson of Polgarus Studio for your formatting skills. I would not have made it to the finish line without your services.

While there is so much time and energy that goes *inside* the book, it is the *outside* that is front and centre and attracts readers. Hence, a huge thank-you to the Damonza team for their time and energy in creating this phenomenal book cover.

In closing, thank you, the reader, for giving me this opportunity to share a part of myself through this book. My greatest hope is that it motivates you to find or create buzzwords that inspire you to be your best self and drive you forward to touch this world in your own positive, proactive, and amazing way.

RESOURCES

These are just a few of the many books that have educated, inspired, and motivated me, and I want to share them with you.

Body

Aging: Fight It with the Blood Type Diet by Dr. Peter J. D'Adamo

Allergies: Fight Them with the Blood Type Diet by Dr. Peter J. D'Adamo

Arthritis: Fight It with the Blood Type Diet by Dr. Peter J. D'Adamo

Breath: The New Science of a Lost Art by James Nestor

Cancer: Fight It with the Blood Type Diet by Dr. Peter J. D'Adamo

Cardiovascular Disease: Fight It with the Blood Type Diet by Dr. Peter J. D'Adamo

Diabetes: Fight It with the Blood Type Diet by Dr. Peter J. D'Adamo

Eat Right 4 Your Type by Dr. Peter J. D'Adamo

Fatigue: Fight It with the Blood Type Diet by Dr. Peter J. D'Adamo

The Good Gut: Taking Control of Your Weight, Your Mood, and Your Long-Term Health by Justin and Erica Sonnenburg

Healthy Beauty: Your Guide to Ingredients to Avoid and Products You Can Trust by Samuel S. Epstein and Randall Fitzgerald

An Inconvenient Sequel: Truth to Power: Your Action Handbook to Learn the Science, Find Your Voice and Help Solve the Climate Crisis by Al Gore

Live Pain-Free: Eliminate Chronic Pain without Drugs or Surgery by Lee Albert, NMT

Live Right 4 Your Type by Dr. Peter J. D'Adamo

Menopause: Manage Its Symptoms with the Blood Type Diet by Dr. Peter J. D'Adamo

Natural Cures "They" Don't Want You to Know About by Kevin Trudeau

The Sacred Balance: Rediscovering Our Place in Nature by David Suzuki

The Science of the Sacred by Nicole Redvers, ND

Mind

21 Things You May Not Know About the Indian Act: Helping Canadians Make Reconciliation with Indigenous Peoples a Reality by Bob Joseph

Across That Bridge: Life Lessons and a Vision for Change by John Lewis

The Bellwether Effect: Stop Following, Start Inspiring! By Lance Secretan

Big Green Purse: Use Your Spending Power to Create a Cleaner, Greener World by Diane MacEachern

The Bully, the Bullied, and the Bystander by Barbara Coloroso

The Dance of Anger: A Woman's Guide to Changing the Patterns of Intimate Relationships by Harriet Lerner, PhD

Emotional Intelligence: Why It Can Matter More Than IQ by Daniel Goleman

From Where I Stand: Rebuilding Indigenous Nations for a Stronger Canada by Jody Wilson-Raybould

How to Be an Antiracist by Ibram X. Kendi

How We Did It: The Subban Plan for Success in Hockey, School and Life by Karl Subban and Scott Colby

The Last Lecture by Randy Pausch and Jeffrey Zaslow

Life's Greatest Lessons: 20 Things That Matter by Hal Urban

The Little Book of Mindfulness: 10 Minutes a Day to Less Stress, More Peace by Dr. Patrizia Collard

Outliers: The Story of Success by Malcolm Gladwell

The Power of Kindness: Why Empathy Is Essential in Everyday Life by Brian Goldman, MD

Shalom in the Home: Smart Advice for a Peaceful Life by Rabbi Shmuley Boteach

Tuesdays with Morrie by Mitch Albom

The Year of Less: How I Stopped Shopping, Gave Away My Belongings, and Discovered Life Is Worth More Than Anything You Can Buy in a Store by Cait Flanders

Spirit

7 Lessons from Heaven: How Dying Taught Me to Live a Joy-Filled Life by Mary C. Neal, MD
Are You There, God? It's Me, Margaret by Judy Blume
Becoming by Michelle Obama
Daring Greatly: How the Courage to Be Vulnerable Transforms the Way We Live, Love, Parent, and Lead by Brené Brown
GuRu by RuPaul
Looks Like Daylight: Voices of Indigenous Kids by Deborah Ellis
Notes to Myself: My Struggle to Become a Person by Hugh Prather
Plain and Simple: A Woman's Journey to the Amish by Sue Bender
The Rainbow Comes and Goes: A Mother and Son on Life, Love, and Loss by Anderson Cooper and Gloria Vanderbilt
The Road Less Traveled: A New Psychology of Love, Traditional Values and Spiritual Growth by M. Scott Peck
Siddhartha by Hermann Hesse
The Simple Abundance Journal of Gratitude by Sarah Ban Breathnach
What I Know for Sure by Oprah Winfrey
With God Nothing Is Impossible: A Canadian Life by Murray Dryden

ABOUT THE AUTHOR

Glori Gage is a Canadian singer, songwriter, and now author. She grew up in Toronto, starting her singing career on a backyard swing and ultimately gracing the stage as part of the ensemble with the acclaimed Stratford Festival's production of *The Mikado*. The production toured Canada and the United States with a rewarding run at the Virginia Theatre on Broadway, New York, and the Old Vic Theatre in London, England. Glori's love of music has extended to recording the "Treasured Memories" music series, a collection of four CDs in a style best described as gentle renderings of timeless classics. She also wrote and released two original songs *Things You Do* and *Heart of Hearts*.

Glori has always believed that one of the greatest forms of education is life itself, by living in the moment and listening closely to the many lessons life has to offer. Through her love of philosophy and the written word, she now adds author to her accomplishments, which was motivated by her extensive journaling and desire to help others.

When she is not writing, reading a good book, or trying a new recipe, she is wearing a pair of old, oversized coveralls and tending to her beloved gardens. Glori lives in north Toronto with her husband.

NOTES

Manufactured by Amazon.ca
Bolton, ON